For Brian Friel

Contents

PART ONE

The Underground	*page* 13
La Toilette	14
Sloe Gin	15
Away from it All	16
Chekhov on Sakhalin	18
Sandstone Keepsake	20
Shelf Life	21
1 Granite Chip	21
2 Old Smoothing Iron	21
3 Old Pewter	22
4 Iron Spike	23
5 Stone from Delphi	24
6 A Snowshoe	24
A Migration	25
Last Look	28
Remembering Malibu	30
Making Strange	32
The Birthplace	34
Changes	36
An Ulster Twilight	38
A Bat on the Road	40
A Hazel Stick for Catherine Ann	42
A Kite for Michael and Christopher	44
The Railway Children	45
Sweetpea	46
An Aisling in the Burren	47
Widgeon	48
Sheelagh na Gig	49
The Loaning	51
The Sandpit	53
The King of the Ditchbacks	56

PART TWO: STATION ISLAND

Station Island   *page* 61

PART THREE: SWEENEY REDIVIVUS

The First Gloss   97
Sweeney Redivivus   98
Unwinding   99
In the Beech   100
The First Kingdom   101
The First Flight   102
Drifting Off   104
Alerted   106
The Cleric   107
The Hermit   109
The Master   110
The Scribes   111
A Waking Dream   112
In the Chestnut Tree   113
Sweeney's Returns   114
Holly   115
An Artist   116
The Old Icons   117
In Illo Tempore   118
On the Road   119

Notes   122

PART ONE

The Underground

There we were in the vaulted tunnel running,
You in your going-away coat speeding ahead
And me, me then like a fleet god gaining
Upon you before you turned to a reed

Or some new white flower japped with crimson
As the coat flapped wild and button after button
Sprang off and fell in a trail
Between the Underground and the Albert Hall.

Honeymooning, moonlighting, late for the Proms,
Our echoes die in that corridor and now
I come as Hansel came on the moonlit stones
Retracing the path back, lifting the buttons

To end up in a draughty lamplit station
After the trains have gone, the wet track
Bared and tensed as I am, all attention
For your step following and damned if I look back.

La Toilette

The white towelling bathrobe
ungirdled, the hair still wet,
first coldness of the underbreast
like a ciborium in the palm.

Our bodies are the temples
of the Holy Ghost. Remember?
And the little, fitted, deep-slit drapes
on and off the holy vessels

regularly? And the chasuble
so deftly hoisted? But vest yourself
in the word you taught me
and the stuff I love: slub silk.

Sloe Gin

The clear weather of juniper
darkened into winter.
She fed gin to sloes
and sealed the glass container.

When I unscrewed it
I smelled the disturbed
tart stillness of a bush
rising through the pantry.

When I poured it
it had a cutting edge
and flamed
like Betelgeuse.

I drink to you
in smoke-mirled, blue-black,
polished sloes, bitter
and dependable.

Away from it All

A cold steel fork
pried the tank water
and forked up a lobster:
articulated twigs, a rainy stone
the colour of sunk munitions.

In full view of the strand,
the sea wind spitting on the big window,
we plunged and reddened it,
then sat for hours in conclave
over the last of the claws.

It was twilight, twilight, twilight
as the questions hopped and rooted.
It was oarsmen's backs and oars
hauled against and lifting.
And more power to us, my friend,

hard at it over the dregs,
laying in in earnest
as the sea darkens
and whitens and darkens
and quotations start to rise

like rehearsed alibis:
I was stretched between contemplation
of a motionless point
and the command to participate
actively in history.

'*Actively?* What do you mean?'
The light at the rim of the sea
is rendered down to a fine
graduation, somewhere between
balance and inanition.

And I still cannot clear my head
of lives in their element
on the cobbled floor of that tank
and the hampered one, out of water,
fortified and bewildered.

Chekhov on Sakhalin

for Derek Mahon

So, he would pay his 'debt to medicine'.
But first he drank cognac by the ocean
With his back to all he travelled north to face.
His head was swimming free as the troikas

Of Tyumin, he looked down from the rail
Of his thirty years and saw a mile
Into himself as if he were clear water:
Lake Baikhal from the deckrail of the steamer.

That far north, Siberia was south.
Should it have been an ulcer in the mouth,
The cognac that the Moscow literati
Packed off with him to a penal colony –

Him, born, you may say, under the counter?
At least that meant he knew its worth. No cantor
In full throat by the iconostasis
Got holier joy than he got from that glass

That shone and warmed like diamonds warming
On some pert young cleavage in a salon,
Inviolable and affronting.
He felt the glass go cold in the midnight sun.

When he staggered up and smashed it on the stones
It rang as clearly as the convicts' chains
That haunted him. In the months to come
It rang on like the burden of his freedom

To try for the right tone – not tract, not thesis –
And walk away from floggings. He who thought to squeeze
His slave's blood out and waken the free man
Shadowed a convict guide through Sakhalin.

Sandstone Keepsake

It is a kind of chalky russet
solidified gourd, sedimentary
and so reliably dense and bricky
I often clasp it and throw it from hand to hand.

It was ruddier, with an underwater
hint of contusion, when I lifted it,
wading a shingle beach on Inishowen.
Across the estuary light after light

came on silently round the perimeter
of the camp. A stone from Phlegethon,
bloodied on the bed of hell's hot river?
Evening frost and the salt water

made my hand smoke, as if I'd plucked the heart
that damned Guy de Montfort to the boiling flood –
but not really, though I remembered
his victim's heart in its casket, long venerated.

Anyhow, there I was with the wet red stone
in my hand, staring across at the watch-towers
from my free state of image and allusion,
swooped on, then dropped by trained binoculars:

a silhouette not worth bothering about,
out for the evening in scarf and waders
and not about to set times wrong or right,
stooping along, one of the venerators.

Shelf Life

1 *Granite Chip*

Houndstooth stone. Aberdeen of the mind.

Saying *An union in the cup I'll throw*
I have hurt my hand, pressing it hard around
this bit hammered off Joyce's Martello
Tower, this flecked insoluble brilliant

I keep but feel little in common with –
a kind of stone age circumcising knife,
a Calvin edge in my complaisant pith.
Granite is jaggy, salty, punitive

and exacting. *Come to me*, it says
all you who labour and are burdened, I
will not refresh you. And it adds, *Seize*
the day. And, *You can take me or leave me*.

2 *Old Smoothing Iron*

Often I watched her lift it
from where its compact wedge
rode the back of the stove
like a tug at anchor.

To test its heat by ear
she spat in its iron face
or held it up next her cheek
to divine the stored danger.

Soft thumps on the ironing board.
Her dimpled angled elbow
and intent stoop
as she aimed the smoothing iron

like a plane into linen,
like the resentment of women.
To work, her dumb lunge says,
is to move a certain mass

through a certain distance,
is to pull your weight and feel
exact and equal to it.
Feel dragged upon. And buoyant.

3 *Old Pewter*

Not the age of silver, more a slither
of illiteracy under rafters:
a dented hand-me-down old smoky plate
full of blizzards, sullied and temperate.

I love unshowy pewter, my soft option
when it comes to the metals – next to solder
that weeps at the touch of a hot iron;
doleful and placid as a gloss-barked alder

reflected in the nebulous lid of a pool
where they thought I had drowned one winter day
a stone's throw from the house, when the whole
country was mist and I hid deliberately.

Glimmerings are what the soul's composed of.
Fogged-up challenges, far conscience-glitters
and hang-dog, half-truth earnests of true love.
And a whole late-flooding thaw of ancestors.

4 Iron Spike

So like a harrow pin
I hear harness creaks and the click
of stones in a ploughed-up field.
But it was the age of steam

at Eagle Pond, New Hampshire,
when this rusted spike I found there
was aimed and driven in
to fix a cog on the line.

What guarantees things keeping
if a railway can be lifted
like a long briar out of ditch growth?
I felt I had come on myself

in the grassy silent path
where I drew the iron like a thorn
or a word I had thought my own
out of a stranger's mouth.

And the sledge-head that sank it
with a last opaque report
deep into the creosoted
sleeper, where is that?

And the sweat-cured haft?
Ask the ones on the buggy,
inaudible and upright
and sped along without shadows.

5 Stone from Delphi

To be carried back to the shrine some dawn
when the sea spreads its far sun-crops to the south
and I make a morning offering again:
that I may escape the miasma of spilled blood,
govern the tongue, fear hybris, fear the god
until he speaks in my untrammelled mouth.

6 A Snowshoe

The loop of a snowshoe hangs on a wall
in my head, in a room that is drift-still:
it is like a brushed longhand character,
a hieroglyph for all the realms of whisper.

It was to follow the snow goose of a word
I left the room after an amorous blizzard
and climbed up attic stairs like a somnambulist,
furred and warm-blooded, scuffling the snow-crust.

Then I sat there writing, imagining in silence
sounds like love sounds after long abstinence,
eager and absorbed and capable
under the sign of a snowshoe on a wall.

The loop of the snowshoe, like an old-time kite,
lifts away in a wind and is lost to sight.
Now I sit blank as gradual morning brightens
its distancing, inviolate expanse.

[24]

A Migration

About a mile above
and beyond our place,
in a house with a leaking roof
and cracked dormer windows
Brigid came to live
with her mother and sisters.

So for months after that
she slept in a crowded bed
under the branch-whipped slates,
bewildered night after night
by starts of womanhood,
and a dream troubled her head

of a ship's passenger lounge
where empty bottles rolled
at every slow plunge
and lift, a weeping child
kept weeping, and a strange
flowing black taxi pulled

into a bombed station.
She would waken to the smell
of baby clothes and children
who snuggled tight, and the small
dormer with no curtain
beginning to go pale.

Windfalls lay at my feet
those days, clandestine winds
stirred in our lyric wood:
restive, quick and silent
the deer of poetry stood
in pools of lucent sound

ready to scare,
as morning and afternoon
Brigid and her sisters
came jangling along, down
the steep hill for water,
and laboured up again.

Familiars! A trail
of spillings in the dust,
unsteady white enamel
buckets looming. Their ghosts,
like their names, called from the hill
to 'Hurry', hurry past,

a spill of syllables.
I knew the story then.
Ferry Glasgow–Belfast,
then to the Dublin train
with their cases and boxes,
pram and cassette machine,

and then they miss the bus,
their last Wicklow connection –
the young ones scared and cross
in the lit bus station,
the mother at a loss.
And so in desperation

they start out for the suburbs
and into the small hours.
How it sweetens and disturbs
as they make their homesick tour,
a moonlight flit, street arabs,
the mother and her daughters

walking south through the land
past neon garages,
night lights haloed on blinds,
padlocked entries, bridges
swelling over a kind
mutter of streams, then trees

start filling the sky
and the estates thin out,
lamps are spaced more widely
until a cold moonlight
shows Wicklow's mountainy
black skyline, and they sit.

They change the cassette
but now the battery's gone.
They cannot raise a note.
When the first drops of rain
spit in the dark, Brigid
gets up and says, 'Come on.'

Last Look

in memoriam E.G.

We came upon him, stilled
and oblivious,
gazing into a field
of blossoming potatoes,
his trouser bottoms wet
and flecked with grass seed.
Crowned blunt-headed weeds
that flourished in the verge
flailed against our car
but he seemed not to hear
in his long watchfulness
by the clifftop fuchsias.

He paid no heed that day,
no more than if he were
sheep's wool on barbed wire
or an old lock of hay
combed from a passing load
by a bush in the roadside.

He was back in his twenties,
travelling Donegal
in the grocery cart
of *Gallagher and Son*,
Merchant, Publican,
Retail and Import.
Flourbags, nosebags, buckets
of water for the horse
in every whitewashed yard.
Drama between hedges
if he met a Model Ford.

If Niamh had ridden up
to make the wide strand sweet
with inviting Irish,
weaving among hoofbeats
and hoofmarks on the wet
dazzle and blaze,
I think not even she
could have drawn him out
from the covert of his gaze.

Remembering Malibu

for Brian Moore

The Pacific at your door was wilder and colder
than my notion of the Pacific

and that was perfect, for I would have rotted
beside the luke-warm ocean I imagined.

Yet no way was its cold ascetic
as our monk-fished, snowed-into Atlantic;

no beehive hut for you
on the abstract sands of Malibu –

it was early Mondrian and his dunes
misting towards the ideal forms

though the wind and sea neighed loud
as wind and sea noise amplified.

I was there in the flesh
where I'd imagined I might be

and underwent the bluster of the day:
but why would it not come home to me?

Atlantic storms have flensed the cells
on the Great Skellig, the steps cut in the rock

I never climbed
between the graveyard and the boatslip

are welted solid to my instep.
But to rear and kick and cast that shoe –

beside that other western sea
far from the Skelligs, and far, far

from the suck of puddled, wintry ground,
our footsteps filled with blowing sand.

Making Strange

I stood between them,
the one with his travelled intelligence
and tawny containment,
his speech like the twang of a bowstring,

and another, unshorn and bewildered
in the tubs of his wellingtons,
smiling at me for help,
faced with this stranger I'd brought him.

Then a cunning middle voice
came out of the field across the road
saying, 'Be adept and be dialect,
tell of this wind coming past the zinc hut,

call me sweetbriar after the rain
or snowberries cooled in the fog.
But love the cut of this travelled one
and call me also the cornfield of Boaz.

Go beyond what's reliable
in all that keeps pleading and pleading,
these eyes and puddles and stones,
and recollect how bold you were

when I visited you first
with departures you cannot go back on.'
A chaffinch flicked from an ash and next thing
I found myself driving the stranger

through my own country, adept
at dialect, reciting my pride
in all that I knew, that began to make strange
at that same recitation.

The Birthplace

I

The deal table where he wrote, so small and plain,
the single bed a dream of discipline.
And a flagged kitchen downstairs, its mote-slants

of thick light: the unperturbed, reliable
ghost life he carried, with no need to invent.
And high trees round the house, breathed upon

day and night by winds as slow as a cart
coming late from market, or the stir
a fiddle could make in his reluctant heart.

II

That day, we were like one
of his troubled pairs, speechless
until he spoke for them,

haunters of silence at noon
in a deep lane that was sexual
with ferns and butterflies,

scared at our hurt,
throat-sick, heat-struck, driven
into the damp-floored wood

where we made an episode
of ourselves, unforgettable,
unmentionable,

and broke out again like cattle
through bushes, wet and raised,
only yards from the house.

III

Everywhere being nowhere,
who can prove
one place more than another?

We come back emptied,
to nourish and resist
the words of coming to rest:

*birthplace, roofbeam, whitewash,
flagstone, hearth,*
like unstacked iron weights

afloat among galaxies.
Still, was it thirty years ago
I read until first light

for the first time, to finish
The Return of the Native?
The corncrake in the aftergrass

verified himself, and I heard
roosters and dogs, the very same
as if he had written them.

Changes

As you came with me in silence
to the pump in the long grass

I heard much that you could not hear:
the bite of the spade that sank it,

the slithering and grumble
as the mason mixed his mortar,

and women coming with white buckets
like flashes on their ruffled wings.

The cast-iron rims of the lid
clinked as I uncovered it,

something stirred in its mouth.
I had a bird's eye view of a bird,

finch-green, speckly white,
nesting on dry leaves, flattened, still,

suffering the light.
So I roofed the citadel

as gently as I could, and told you
and you gently unroofed it

but where was the bird now?
There was a single egg, pebbly white,

and in the rusted bend of the spout
tail feathers splayed and sat tight.

So tender, I said, 'Remember this.
It will be good for you to retrace this path

when you have grown away and stand at last
at the very centre of the empty city.'

An Ulster Twilight

The bare bulb, a scatter of nails,
Shelved timber, glinting chisels:
In a shed of corrugated iron
Eric Dawson stoops to his plane

At five o'clock on a Christmas Eve.
Carpenter's pencil next, the spoke-shave,
Fretsaw, auger, rasp and awl,
A rub with a rag of linseed oil.

A mile away it was taking shape,
The hulk of a toy battleship,
As waterbuckets iced and frost
Hardened the quiet on roof and post.

Where is he now?
There were fifteen years between us two
That night I strained to hear the bells
Of a sleigh of the mind and heard him pedal

Into our lane, get off at the gable,
Steady his Raleigh bicycle
Against the whitewash, stand to make sure
The house was quiet, knock at the door

And hand his parcel to a peering woman:
'I suppose you thought I was never coming.'
Eric, tonight I saw it all
Like shadows on your workshop wall,

Smelled wood shavings under the bench,
Weighed the cold steel monkey-wrench
In my soft hand, then stood at the road
To watch your wavering tail-light fade

And knew that if we met again
In an Ulster twilight we would begin
And end whatever we might say
In a speech all toys and carpentry,

A doorstep courtesy to shun
Your father's uniform and gun,
But – now that I have said it out –
Maybe none the worse for that.

A Bat on the Road

A batlike soul waking to consciousness of itself in
darkness and secrecy and loneliness.

You would hoist an old hat on the tines of a fork
and trawl the mouth of the bridge for the slight
bat-thump and flutter. Skinny downy webs,

babynails clawing the sweatband . . . But don't
bring it down, don't break its flight again,
don't deny it; this time let it go free.

Follow its bat-flap under the stone bridge,
under the Midland and Scottish Railway
and lose it there in the dark.

Next thing it shadows moonslicked laurels
or skims the lapped net on a tennis court.
Next thing it's ahead of you in the road.

What are you after? You keep swerving off,
flying blind over ashpits and netting wire;
invited by the brush of a word like *peignoir*,

rustles and glimpses, shot silk, the stealth of floods
So close to me I could hear her breathing
and there by the lighted window behind trees

it hangs in creepers matting the brickwork
and now it's a wet leaf blowing in the drive,
now soft-deckled, shadow-convolvulus

by the White Gates. Who would have thought it? At the
   White Gates
She let them do whatever they liked. Cling there
as long as you want. There is nothing to hide.

A Hazel Stick for Catherine Ann

The living mother-of-pearl of a salmon
just out of the water

is gone just like that, but your stick
is kept salmon-silver.

Seasoned and bendy,
it convinces the hand

that what you have you hold
to play with and pose with

and lay about with.
But then too it points back to cattle

and spatter and beating
the bars of a gate –

the very stick we might cut
from your family tree.

The living cobalt of an afternoon
dragonfly drew my eye to it first

and the evening I trimmed it for you
you saw your first glow-worm –

all of us stood round in silence, even you
gigantic enough to darken the sky

for a glow-worm.
And when I poked open the grass

a tiny brightening den lit the eye
in the blunt cut end of your stick.

A Kite for Michael and Christopher

All through that Sunday afternoon
a kite flew above Sunday,
a tightened drumhead, an armful of blown chaff.

I'd seen it grey and slippy in the making,
I'd tapped it when it dried out white and stiff,
I'd tied the bows of newspaper
along its six-foot tail.

But now it was far up like a small black lark
and now it dragged as if the bellied string
were a wet rope hauled upon
to lift a shoal.

My friend says that the human soul
is about the weight of a snipe
yet the soul at anchor there,
the string that sags and ascends,
weigh like a furrow assumed into the heavens.

Before the kite plunges down into the wood
and this line goes useless
take in your two hands, boys, and feel
the strumming, rooted, long-tailed pull of grief.
You were born fit for it.
Stand in here in front of me
and take the strain.

The Railway Children

When we climbed the slopes of the cutting
We were eye-level with the white cups
Of the telegraph poles and the sizzling wires.

Like lovely freehand they curved for miles
East and miles west beyond us, sagging
Under their burden of swallows.

We were small and thought we knew nothing
Worth knowing. We thought words travelled the wires
In the shiny pouches of raindrops,

Each one seeded full with the light
Of the sky, the gleam of the lines, and ourselves
So infinitesimally scaled

We could stream through the eye of a needle.

Sweetpea

'What did Thought do?'
                    'Stuck
a feather in the ground and thought
it would grow a hen.'
                    Rod
by rod we pegged the drill for sweetpea
with light brittle sticks,
twiggy and unlikely in fresh mould,
and stalk by stalk we snipped
the coming blooms.

                    And so when pain
had haircracked her old constant vestal stare
I reached for straws and thought:
seeing the sky through a mat of creepers,
like water in the webs of a green net,
opened a clearing where her heart sang
without caution or embarrassment, once or twice.

An Aisling in the Burren

A time was to come when we yearned
for the eel-drugged flats and dunes
of a northern shore, its dulse and its seabirds,
its divisions of brine-maddened grass
pouring over dykes to secure
the aftermath of the reign of the meek.
That was as much of hope that the purest
and saddest were prepared to allow for.

Out of those scenes she arrived, not from a shell
but licked with the wet cold fires of St Elmo,
angel of the last chance, teaching us
the fish in the rock, the fern's
bewildered tenderness deep in the fissure.

That day the clatter of stones
as we climbed was a sermon
on conscience and healing,
her tears a startling deer
on the site of catastrophe.

Widgeon

for Paul Muldoon

It had been badly shot.
While he was plucking it
he found, he says, the voice box –

like a flute stop
in the broken windpipe –

and blew upon it
unexpectedly
his own small widgeon cries.

Sheelagh na Gig

at Kilpeck

I

We look up at her
hunkered into her angle
under the eaves.

She bears the whole stone burden
on the small of her back and shoulders
and pinioned elbows,

the astute mouth, the gripping fingers
saying push, push hard,
push harder.

As the hips go high
her big tadpole forehead
is rounded out in sunlight.

And here beside her are two birds,
a rabbit's head, a ram's,
a mouth devouring heads.

II

Her hands holding herself
are like hands in an old barn
holding a bag open.

I was outside looking in
at its lapped and supple mouth
running grain.

[49]

I looked up under the thatch
at the dark mouth and eye
of a bird's nest or a rat hole,

smelling the rose on the wall,
mildew, an earthen floor,
the warm depth of the eaves.

And then one night in the yard
I stood still under heavy rain
wearing the bag like a caul.

III

We look up to her,
her ring-fort eyes,
her little slippy shoulders,

her nose incised and flat,
and feel light-headed looking up.
She is twig-boned, saddle-sexed,

grown-up, grown ordinary,
seeming to say,
'Yes, look at me to your heart's content

but look at every other thing.'
And here is a leaper in a kilt,
two figures kissing,

a mouth with sprigs,
a running hart, two fishes,
a damaged beast with an instrument.

The Loaning

I

As I went down the loaning
the wind shifting in the hedge was like
an old one's whistling speech. And I knew
I was in the limbo of lost words.

They had flown there from raftered sheds and crossroads,
from the shelter of gable ends and turned-up carts.
I saw them streaming out of birch-white throats
and fluttering above iron bedsteads
until the soul would leave the body.
Then on a day close as a stranger's breath
they rose in smoky clouds on the summer sky
and settled in the uvulae of stones
and the soft lungs of the hawthorn.

Then I knew why from the beginning
the loaning breathed on me, breathed even now
in a shiver of beaded gossamers
and the spit blood of a last few haws and rose-hips.

II

Big voices in the womanless kitchen.
They never lit a lamp in the summertime
but took the twilight as it came
like solemn trees. They sat on in the dark
with their pipes red in their mouths, the talk come down
to *Aye* and *Aye* again and, when the dog shifted,
a curt *There boy!* I closed my eyes
to make the light motes stream behind them
and my head went airy, my chair rode

high and low among branches and the wind
stirred up a rookery in the next long *Aye*.

III

Stand still. You can hear
everything going on. High-tension cables
singing above cattle, tractors, barking dogs,
juggernauts changing gear a mile away.
And always the surface noise of the earth
you didn't know you'd heard till a twig snapped
and a blackbird's startled volubility
stopped short.

          When you are tired or terrified
your voice slips back into its old first place
and makes the sound your shades make there . . .
When Dante snapped a twig in the bleeding wood
a voice sighed out of blood that bubbled up
like sap at the end of green sticks on a fire.

At the click of a cell lock somewhere now
the interrogator steels his *introibo*,
the light motes blaze, a blood-red cigarette
startles the shades, screeching and beseeching.

The Sandpit

1 1946

The first hole neat as a trapdoor
cut into grazing and
cut again as the heft and lift
begin, the plate scrabs field-stones
and a tremor blunts in the shaft
at small come-uppances meeting
the driven edge.
                 Worms and starlight,
mould-balm on the passing cyclist's face.
The rat's nose in the plastered verge
where they walked to clean their boots.

2 The Demobbed Bricklayer

A fence post trimmed and packed
into place, but out of place:
                      the soldier
not a soldier any more and never
quite a soldier, what has he
walked into? This is not the desert
night among cold ambulances,
not the absolute sand
of the world, the sun's whip
and grid –
         this sand,
this lustre in their heavy land
is greedy coppers hammered
in the wishing tree of their talk,
the damp ore of money.
                Freckled
and demobbed, worked on like the soil

he is inhaling, he stands
remembering his trade, the song
of his trowel dressing a brickbat,
the tock and tap of its butt, the plumb-
line's certitude, the merriment
in the spirit level's eye.

3 *The Sand Boom*

A fortune in sand then. Sandpits and sandbeds.
River gravel drying in the brickyards.
Clay-scabbed flints, skimming stones of slate,
sandstone pebbles, birds' eggs of flecked granite
all rattled in the caked iron mouth
of the concrete mixer.
                         The first spadeful I saw
pitched up, the handful of gravel
I flung over the cribs,
until they burn in the fireball
or crumble at the edge of the blast
or drink the rain again on their flattened site,
are bonded and set to register
whatever beams and throbs into the wall.
Like undead grains in a stranded cockle shell.
Boulders listening behind the waterfall.

And this as well:
                    foxgloves and saplings
on the worked-out pit floor, grass on the cracked
earth face, anglers nested in an overgrown
loading bay above the deepened stream.

4 *What the Brick Keeps*

His touch, his daydream of the tanks,
his point of vantage on the scaffolding
over chimneys and close hills at noontime,
the constant sound of hidden river water
the new estate rose up through –
with one chop of the trowel he sent it all
into the brick for ever.
It has not stopped travelling in
in the van of all that followed:
floors hammered down, the pipes' first
gulping flow, phone wires and flags
alive on the gable, a bedhead
thumping quickly, banged doors shaking
the joists, rippling the very roof tank.
And my own hands, the size of a grandchild's,
go in there, cold and wet, and my big gaze
at the sandpit opening by the minute.

The King of the Ditchbacks

for John Montague

I

As if a trespasser
unbolted a forgotten gate
and ripped the growth
tangling its lower bars –

just beyond the hedge
he has opened a dark morse
along the bank,
a crooked wounding

of silent, cobwebbed
grass. If I stop
he stops
like the moon.

He lives in his feet
and ears, weather-eyed,
all pad and listening,
a denless mover.

Under the bridge
his reflection shifts
sideways to the current,
mothy, alluring.

I am haunted
by his stealthy rustling,
the unexpected spoor,
the pollen settling.

II

I was sure I knew him. The time I'd spent obsessively in that upstairs room bringing myself close to him: each entranced hiatus as I chainsmoked and stared out the dormer into the grassy hillside I was laying myself open. He was depending on me as I hung out on the limb of a translated phrase like a youngster dared out on to an alder branch over the whirlpool. Small dreamself in the branches. Dream fears I inclined towards, interrogating:

— Are you the one I ran upstairs to find drowned under running water in the bath?
— The one the mowing machine severed like a hare in the stiff frieze of harvest?
— Whose little bloody clothes we buried in the garden?
— The one who lay awake in darkness a wall's breadth from the troubled hoofs?

After I had dared these invocations, I went back towards the gate to follow him. And my stealth was second nature to me, as if I were coming into my own. I remembered I had been vested for this calling.

III

When I was taken aside that day
I had the sense of election:

they dressed my head in a fishnet
and plaited leafy twigs through meshes

so my vision was a bird's
at the heart of a thicket

[57]

and I spoke as I moved
like a voice from a shaking bush.

King of the ditchbacks,
I went with them obediently

to the edge of a pigeon wood –
deciduous canopy, screened wain of evening

we lay beneath in silence.
No birds came, but I waited

among briars and stones, or whispered
or broke the watery gossamers

if I moved a muscle.
'Come back to us,' they said, 'in harvest,

when we hide in the stooked corn,
when the gundogs can hardly retrieve

what's brought down.' And I saw myself
rising to move in that dissimulation,

top-knotted, masked in sheaves, noting
the fall of birds: a rich young man

leaving everything he had
for a migrant solitude.

PART TWO:

STATION ISLAND

Station Island

I

A hurry of bell-notes
flew over morning hush
and water-blistered cornfields,
an escaped ringing
that stopped as quickly

as it started. *Sunday*,
the silence breathed
and could not settle back
for a man had appeared
at the side of the field

with a bow-saw, held
stiffly up like a lyre.
He moved and stopped to gaze
up into hazel bushes,
angled his saw in,

pulled back to gaze again
and move on to the next.
'I know you, Simon Sweeney,
for an old Sabbath-breaker
who has been dead for years.'

'Damn all you know,' he said,
his eye still on the hedge
and not turning his head.
'I was your mystery man
and am again this morning.

Through gaps in the bushes,
your First Communion face
would watch me cutting timber.
When cut or broken limbs
of trees went yellow, when

woodsmoke sharpened air
or ditches rustled
you sensed my trail there
as if it had been sprayed.
It left you half afraid.

When they bade you listen
in the bedroom dark
to wind and rain in the trees
and think of tinkers camped
under a heeled-up cart

you shut your eyes and saw
a wet axle and spokes
in moonlight, and me
streaming from the shower,
headed for your door.'

Sunlight broke in the hazels,
the quick bell-notes began
a second time. I turned
at another sound:
a crowd of shawled women

were wading the young corn,
their skirts brushing softly.
Their motion saddened morning.
It whispered to the silence,
'Pray for us, pray for us,'

[62]

it conjured through the air
until the field was full
of half-remembered faces,
a loosed congregation
that straggled past and on.

As I drew behind them
I was a fasted pilgrim,
light-headed, leaving home
to face into my station.
'Stay clear of all processions!'

Sweeney shouted at me
but the murmur of the crowd
and their feet slushing through
the tender, bladed growth
opened a drugged path

I was set upon.
I trailed those early-risers
who had fallen into step
before the smokes were up.
The quick bell rang again.

II

I was parked on a high road, listening
to peewits and wind blowing round the car
when something came to life in the driving mirror,

someone walking fast in an overcoat
and boots, bareheaded, big, determined
in his sure haste along the crown of the road

so that I felt myself the challenged one.
The car door slammed. I was suddenly out
face to face with an aggravated man

raving on about nights spent listening for
gun butts to come cracking on the door,
yeomen on the rampage, and his neighbour

among them, hammering home the shape of things.
'Round about here you overtook the women,'
I said, as the thing came clear. 'Your *Lough Derg Pilgrim*

haunts me every time I cross this mountain –
as if I am being followed, or following.
I'm on my road there now to do the station.'

'O holy Jesus Christ, does nothing change?'
His head jerked sharply side to side and up
like a diver surfacing,

then with a look that said, *who is this cub
anyhow*, he took cognizance again
of where he was: the road, the mountain top,

and the air, softened by a shower of rain,
worked on his anger visibly until:
'It is a road you travel on your own.

I who learned to read in the reek of flax
and smelled hanged bodies rotting on their gibbets
and saw their looped slime gleaming from the sacks –

hard-mouthed Ribbonmen and Orange bigots
made me into the old fork-tongued turncoat
who mucked the byre of their politics.

If times were hard, I could be hard too.
I made the traitor in me sink the knife.
And maybe there's a lesson there for you,

whoever you are, wherever you come out of,
for though there's something natural in your smile
there's something in it strikes me as defensive.'

'I have no mettle for the angry role,'
I said. 'I come from County Derry,
born in earshot of an Hibernian hall

where a band of Ribbonmen played hymns to Mary.
By then the brotherhood was a frail procession
staggering home drunk on Patrick's Day

in collarettes and sashes fringed with green.
Obedient strains like theirs tuned me first
and not that harp of unforgiving iron

[65]

the Fenians strung. A lot of what you wrote
I heard and did: this Lough Derg station,
flax-pullings, dances, summer crossroads chat

and the shaky local voice of education.
All that. And always, Orange drums.
And neighbours on the roads at night with guns.'

'I know, I know, I know, I know,' he said,
'but you have to try to make sense of what comes.
Remember everything and keep your head.'

'The alders in the hedge,' I said, 'mushrooms,
dark-clumped grass where cows or horses dunged,
the cluck when pith-lined chestnut shells split open

in your hand, the melt of shells corrupting,
old jampots in a drain clogged up with mud –'
But now Carleton was interrupting:

'All this is like a trout kept in a spring
or maggots sown in wounds –
another life that cleans our element.

We are earthworms of the earth, and all that
has gone through us is what will be our trace.'
He turned on his heel when he was saying this

and headed up the road at the same hard pace.

III

I knelt. Hiatus. Habit's afterlife . . .
I was back among bead clicks and the murmurs
from inside confessionals, side altars
where candles died insinuating slight

intimate smells of wax at body heat.
There was an active, wind-stilled hush, as if
in a shell the listened-for ocean stopped
and a tide rested and sustained the roof.

A seaside trinket floated then and idled
in vision, like phosphorescent weed,
a toy grotto with seedling mussel shells
and cockles glued in patterns over it,

pearls condensed from a child invalid's breath
into a shimmering ark, my house of gold
that housed the snowdrop weather of her death
long ago. I would stow away in the hold

of our big oak sideboard and forage for it
laid past in its tissue paper for good.
It was like touching birds' eggs, robbing the nest
of the word *wreath*, as kept and dry and secret

as her name which they hardly ever spoke
but was a white bird trapped inside me
beating scared wings when *Health of the Sick*
fluttered its *pray for us* in the litany.

A cold draught blew under the kneeling boards.
I thought of walking round
and round a space utterly empty,
utterly a source, like the idea of sound;

like an absence stationed in the swamp-fed air
above a ring of walked-down grass and rushes
where we once found the bad carcass and scrags of hair
of our dog that had disappeared weeks before.

IV

Blurred swimmings as I faced the sun, my back
to the stone pillar and the iron cross,
ready to say the dream words *I renounce* . . .

Blurred oval prints of newly ordained faces,
'Father' pronounced with a fawning relish,
the sunlit tears of parents being blessed.

I met a young priest, glossy as a blackbird,
as if he had stepped from his anointing
a moment ago: his purple stole and cord

or cincture tied loosely, his polished shoes
unexpectedly secular beneath
a pleated, lace-hemmed alb of linen cloth.

His name had lain undisturbed for years
like an old bicycle wheel in a ditch
ripped at last from under jungling briars,

wet and perished. My arms were open wide
but I could not say the words. 'The rain forest,' he said,
'you've never seen the like of it. I lasted

only a couple of years. Bare-breasted
women and rat-ribbed men. Everything wasted.
I rotted like a pear. I sweated masses . . .'

His breath came short and shorter. 'In long houses
I raised the chalice above headdresses.
In hoc signo . . . On that abandoned

mission compound, my vocation
is a steam off drenched creepers.'
I had broken off from the renunciation

while he was speaking, to clear the way
for other pilgrims queueing to get started.
'I'm older now than you when you went away,'

I ventured, feeling a strange reversal.
'I never could see you on the foreign missions.
I could only see you on a bicycle,

a clerical student home for the summer
doomed to the decent thing. Visiting neighbours.
Drinking tea and praising home-made bread.

Something in them would be ratified
when they saw you at the door in your black suit,
arriving like some sort of holy mascot.

You gave too much relief, you raised a siege
the world had laid against their kitchen grottoes
hung with holy pictures and crucifixes.'

'And you,' he faltered, 'what are you doing here
but the same thing? What possessed you?
I at least was young and unaware

that what I thought was chosen was convention.
But all this you were clear of you walked into
over again. And the god has, as they say, withdrawn.

[70]

What are you doing, going through these motions?
Unless . . . Unless . . .' Again he was short of breath
and his whole fevered body yellowed and shook.

'Unless you are here taking the last look.'
Suddenly where he stood was bare as the roads
we both had grown up beside, where a sick man

had taken his last look one drizzly evening
when steam rose like the first breath of spring,
a knee-deep mist I waded silently

behind him, on his circuits, visiting.

V

An old man's hands, like soft paws rowing forward,
groped for and warded off the air ahead.
Barney Murphy shuffled on the concrete.
Master Murphy. I heard the weakened voice
bulling in sudden rage all over again
and fell in behind, my eyes fixed on his heels
like a man lifting swathes at a mower's heels.
His sockless feet were like the dried broad bean
that split its stitches in the display jar
high on a window in the old classroom,
white as shy faces in the classroom door.
'Master,' those elders whispered, 'I wonder, master . . .',
rustling envelopes, proffering them, withdrawing,
and 'Master' I repeated to myself
so that he stopped but did not turn or move,
his shoulders gone quiet and small, his head
vigilant in the cold gusts off the lough.
I moved ahead and faced him, shook his hand.

Above the winged collar, his mottled face
went distant in a smile as the voice
readied itself and husked and scraped, 'Good man,
good man yourself,' before it lapsed again
in the limbo and dry urn of the larynx.
The adam's apple in its weathered sac
worked like the plunger of a pump in drought
but yielded nothing to help the helpless smile.
Morning field smells came past on the wind,
the sex-cut of sweetbriar after rain,

[72]

new-mown meadow hay, bird's nests filled with leaves.
'You'd have thought that Anahorish School
was purgatory enough for any man,'
I said. 'You've done your station.'
Then a little trembling happened and his breath
rushed the air softly as scythes in his lost meadows.
'Birch trees have overgrown Leitrim Moss,
dairy herds are grazing where the school was
and the school garden's loose black mould is grass.'
He was gone with that and I was faced wrong way
into more pilgrims absorbed in this exercise.
As I stood among their whispers and bare feet
the mists of all the mornings I set out
for Latin classes with him, face to face,
refreshed me. *Mensa, mensa, mensam*
sang in the air like a busy whetstone.

'We'll go some day to my uncle's farm at Toome –'
Another master spoke. '*For what is the great
moving power and spring of verse? Feeling, and
in particular, love.* When I went last year
I drank three cups of water from the well.
It was very cold. It stung me in the ears.
You should have met him –' Coming in as usual
with the rubbed quotation and his cocked bird's eye
dabbing for detail. *When you're on the road
give lifts to people, you'll always learn something.*
There he went, in his belted gaberdine,
and after him, a third fosterer,
slack-shouldered and clear-eyed: 'Sure I might have known
once I had made the pad, you'd be after me
sooner or later. Forty-two years on
and you've got no farther! But after that again,
where else would you go? Iceland, maybe? Maybe the
  Dordogne?'

[73]

And then the parting shot. 'In my own day
the odd one came here on the hunt for women.'

VI

Freckle-face, fox-head, pod of the broom,
Catkin-pixie, little fern-swish:
Where did she arrive from?
Like a wish wished
And gone, her I chose at 'secrets'
And whispered to. When we were playing houses.
I was sunstruck at the basilica door –
A stillness far away, a space, a dish,
A blackened tin and knocked over stool –
Like a tramped neolithic floor
Uncovered among dunes where the bent grass
Whispers on like reeds about Midas's
Secrets, secrets. I shut my ears to the bell.
Head hugged. Eyes shut. Leaf ears. *Don't tell. Don't tell.*

A stream of pilgrims answering the bell
Trailed up the steps as I went down them
Towards the bottle-green, still
Shade of an oak. Shades of the Sabine farm
On the beds of Saint Patrick's Purgatory.
Late summer, country distance, not an air:
Loosen the toga for wine and poetry
Till Phoebus returning routs the morning star.
As a somnolent hymn to Mary rose
I felt an old pang that bags of grain
And the sloped shafts of forks and hoes
Once mocked me with, at my own long virgin
Fasts and thirsts, my nightly shadow feasts,
Haunting the granaries of words like *breasts.*

As if I knelt for years at a keyhole
Mad for it, and all that ever opened
Was the breathed-on grille of a confessional
Until that night I saw her honey-skinned
Shoulder-blades and the wheatlands of her back
Through the wide keyhole of her keyhole dress
And a window facing the deep south of luck
Opened and I inhaled the land of kindness.
As little flowers that were all bowed and shut
By the night chills rise on their stems and open
As soon as they have felt the touch of sunlight,
So I revived in my own wilting powers
And my heart flushed, like somebody set free.
Translated, given, under the oak tree.

VII

I had come to the edge of the water,
soothed by just looking, idling over it
as if it were a clear barometer

or a mirror, when his reflection
did not appear but I sensed a presence
entering into my concentration

on not being concentrated as he spoke
my name. And though I was reluctant
I turned to meet his face and the shock

is still in me at what I saw. His brow
was blown open above the eye and blood
had dried on his neck and cheek. 'Easy now,'

he said, 'it's only me. You've seen men as raw
after a football match . . . What time it was
when I was wakened up I still don't know

but I heard this knocking, knocking, and it
scared me, like the phone in the small hours,
so I had the sense not to put on the light

but looked out from behind the curtain.
I saw two customers on the doorstep
and an old landrover with the doors open

parked on the street so I let the curtain drop;
but they must have been waiting for it to move
for they shouted to come down into the shop.

She started to cry then and roll round the bed,
lamenting and lamenting to herself,
not even asking who it was. "Is your head

astray, or what's come over you?" I roared, more
to bring myself to my senses
than out of any real anger at her

for the knocking shook me, the way they kept it up,
and her whingeing and half-screeching made it worse.
All the time they were shouting, "Shop!

Shop!" so I pulled on my shoes and a sportscoat
and went back to the window and called out,
"What do you want? Could you quieten the racket

or I'll not come down at all." "There's a child not well.
Open up and see what you have got – pills
or a powder or something in a bottle,"

one of them said. He stepped back off the footpath
so I could see his face in the street lamp
and when the other moved I knew them both.

But bad and all as the knocking was, the quiet
hit me worse. She was quiet herself now,
lying dead still, whispering to watch out.

At the bedroom door I switched on the light.
"It's odd they didn't look for a chemist.
Who are they anyway at this time of the night?"

[78]

she asked me, with the eyes standing in her head.
"I know them to see," I said, but something
made me reach and squeeze her hand across the bed

before I went downstairs into the aisle
of the shop. I stood there, going weak
in the legs. I remember the stale smell

of cooked meat or something coming through
as I went to open up. From then on
you know as much about it as I do.'

'Did they say nothing?' 'Nothing. What would they say?'
'Were they in uniform? Not masked in any way?'
'They were barefaced as they would be in the day,

shites thinking they were the be-all and the end-all.'
'Not that it is any consolation,
but they were caught,' I told him, 'and got jail.'

Big-limbed, decent, open-faced, he stood
forgetful of everything now except
whatever was welling up in his spoiled head,

beginning to smile. 'You've put on weight
since you did your courting in that big Austin
you got the loan of on a Sunday night.'

Through life and death he had hardly aged.
There always was an athlete's cleanliness
shining off him and except for the ravaged

forehead and the blood, he was still that same
rangy midfielder in a blue jersey
and starched pants, the one stylist on the team,

the perfect, clean, unthinkable victim.
'Forgive the way I have lived indifferent –
forgive my timid circumspect involvement,'

I surprised myself by saying. 'Forgive
my eye,' he said, 'all that's above my head.'
And then a stun of pain seemed to go through him

and he trembled like a heatwave and faded.

VIII

Black water. White waves. Furrows snowcapped.
A magpie flew from the basilica
and staggered in the granite airy space
I was staring into, on my knees
at the hard mouth of St Brigid's Bed.
I came to and there at the bed's stone hub
was my archaeolgist, very like himself,
with his scribe's face smiling its straight-lipped smile,
starting at the sight of me with the same old
pretence of amazement, so that the wing
of woodkerne's hair fanned down over his brow.
And then as if a shower were blackening
already blackened stubble, the dark weather
of his unspoken pain came over him.
A pilgrim bent and whispering on his rounds
inside the bed passed between us slowly.

'Those dreamy stars that pulsed across the screen
beside you in the ward – your heartbeats, Tom, I mean –
scared me the way they stripped things naked.
My banter failed too early in that visit.
I could not take my eyes off the machine.
I had to head back straight away to Dublin,
guilty and empty, feeling I had said nothing
and that, as usual, I had somehow broken
covenants, and failed an obligation.
I half-knew we would never meet again . . .
Did our long gaze and last handshake contain
nothing to appease that recognition?'

'Nothing at all. But familiar stone
had me half-numbed to face the thing alone.
I loved my still-faced archaeology.
The small crab-apple physiognomies
on high crosses, carved heads in abbeys . . .
Why else dig in for years in that hard place
in a muck of bigotry under the walls
picking through shards and Williamite cannon balls?
But all that we just turned to banter too.
I felt that I should have seen far more of you
and maybe would have – but dead at thirty-two!
Ah poet, lucky poet, tell me why
what seemed deserved and promised passed me by?'

I could not speak. I saw a hoard of black
basalt axe heads, smooth as a beetle's back,
a cairn of stone force that might detonate,
the eggs of danger. And then I saw a face
he had once given me, a plaster cast
of an abbess, done by the Gowran master,
mild-mouthed and cowled, a character of grace.
'Your gift will be a candle in our house.'
But he had gone when I looked to meet his eyes
and hunkering instead there in his place
was a bleeding, pale-faced boy, plastered in mud.
'The red-hot pokers blazed a lovely red
in Jerpoint the Sunday I was murdered,'
he said quietly. 'Now do you remember?
You were there with poets when you got the word
and stayed there with them, while your own flesh and
    blood
was carted to Bellaghy from the Fews.
They showed more agitation at the news
than you did.'

'But they were getting crisis
first-hand, Colum, they had happened in on
live sectarian assassination.
I was dumb, encountering what was destined.'
And so I pleaded with my second cousin.
'I kept seeing a grey stretch of Lough Beg
and the strand empty at daybreak.
I felt like the bottom of a dried-up lake.'

'You saw that, and you wrote that – not the fact.
You confused evasion and artistic tact.
The Protestant who shot me through the head
I accuse directly, but indirectly, you
who now atone perhaps upon this bed
for the way you whitewashed ugliness and drew
the lovely blinds of the *Purgatorio*
and saccharined my death with morning dew.'

Then I seemed to waken out of sleep
among more pilgrims whom I did not know
drifting to the hostel for the night.

IX

'My brain dried like spread turf, my stomach
Shrank to a cinder and tightened and cracked.
Often I was dogs on my own track
Of blood on wet grass that I could have licked.
Under the prison blanket, an ambush
Stillness I felt safe in settled round me.
Street lights came on in small towns, the bomb flash
Came before the sound, I saw country
I knew from Glenshane down to Toome
And heard a car I could make out years away
With me in the back of it like a white-faced groom,
A hit-man on the brink, emptied and deadly.
When the police yielded my coffin, I was light
As my head when I took aim.'

                            This voice from blight
And hunger died through the black dorm:
There he was, laid out with a drift of mass cards
At his shrouded feet. Then the firing party's
Volley in the yard. I saw woodworm
In gate posts and door jambs, smelt mildew
From the byre loft where he watched and hid
From fields his draped coffin would raft through.
Unquiet soul, they should have buried you
In the bog where you threw your first grenade,
Where only helicopters and curlews
Make their maimed music, and sphagnum moss
Could teach you its medicinal repose
Until, when the weasel whistles on its tail,
No other weasel will obey its call.

[84]

I dreamt and drifted. All seemed to run to waste
As down a swirl of mucky, glittering flood
Strange polyp floated like a huge corrupt
Magnolia bloom, surreal as a shed breast,
My softly awash and blanching self-disgust.
And I cried among night waters, 'I repent
My unweaned life that kept me competent
To sleepwalk with connivance and mistrust.'
Then, like a pistil growing from the polyp,
A lighted candle rose and steadied up
Until the whole bright-masted thing retrieved
A course and the currents it had gone with
Were what it rode and showed. No more adrift,
My feet touched bottom and my heart revived.

Then something round and clear
And mildly turbulent, like a bubbleskin
Or a moon in smoothly rippled lough water
Rose in a cobwebbed space: the molten
Inside-sheen of an instrument
Revolved its polished convexes full
Upon me, so close and brilliant
I pitched backwards in a headlong fall.
And then it was the clarity of waking
To sunlight and a bell and gushing taps
In the next cubicle. Still there for the taking!
The old brass trumpet with its valves and stops
I found once in loft thatch, a mystery
I shied from then for I thought such trove beyond me.

'I hate how quick I was to know my place.
I hate where I was born, hate everything
That made me biddable and unforthcoming,'
I mouthed at my half-composed face
In the shaving mirror, like somebody

Drunk in the bathroom during a party,
Lulled and repelled by his own reflection.
As if the cairnstone could defy the cairn.
As if the eddy could reform the pool.
As if a stone swirled under a cascade,
Eroded and eroding in its bed,
Could grind itself down to a different core.
Then I thought of the tribe whose dances never fail
For they keep dancing till they sight the deer.

X

Morning stir in the hostel. A pot
hooked on forged links. Soot flakes. Plumping water.
The open door letting in sunlight.
Hearthsmoke rambling and a thud of earthenware

drumming me back until I saw the mug
beyond my reach on its high shelf, the one
patterned with cornflowers, blue sprig after sprig
repeating round it, as quiet as a milestone,

old and glazed and haircracked. It had stood for years
in its patient sheen and turbulent atoms,
unchallenging, unremembered *lars*
I seemed to waken to and waken from.

When had it not been there? There was one night
when the fit-up actors used it for a prop
and I sat in a dark hall estranged from it
as a couple vowed and called it their loving cup

and held it in our gaze until the curtain
jerked shut with an ordinary noise.
Dipped and glamoured from this translation,
it was restored with all its cornflower haze

still dozing, its parchment glazes fast –
as the otter surfaced once with Ronan's psalter
miraculously unharmed, that had been lost
a day and a night under lough water.

[87]

And so the saint praised God on the lough shore.
The dazzle of the impossible suddenly
blazed across the threshold, a sun-glare
to put out the small hearths of constancy.

XI

As if the prisms of the kaleidoscope
I plunged once in a butt of muddied water
surfaced like a marvellous lightship

and out of its silted crystals a monk's face
that had spoken years ago from behind a grille
spoke again about the need and chance

to salvage everything, to re-envisage
the zenith and glimpsed jewels of any gift
mistakenly abased . . .

What came to nothing could always be replenished.
'Read poems as prayers,' he said, 'and for your penance
translate me something by Juan de la Cruz.'

Returned from Spain to our chapped wilderness,
his consonants aspirate, his forehead shining,
he had made me feel there was nothing to confess.

Now his sandalled passage stirred me on to this:
How well I know that fountain, filling, running,
    although it is the night.

That eternal fountain, hidden away,
I know its haven and its secrecy
    although it is the night.

But not its source because it does not have one,
which is all sources' source and origin
    although it is the night.

No other thing can be so beautiful.
Here the earth and heaven drink their fill
    although it is the night.

So pellucid it never can be muddied,
and I know that all light radiates from it
    although it is the night.

I know no sounding-line can find its bottom,
nobody ford or plumb its deepest fathom
    although it is the night.

And its current so in flood it overspills
to water hell and heaven and all peoples
    although it is the night.

And the current that is generated there,
as far as it wills to, it can flow that far
    although it is the night.

And from these two a third current proceeds
which neither of these two, I know, precedes
    although it is the night.

This eternal fountain hides and splashes
within this living bread that is life to us
    although it is the night.

Hear it calling out to every creature.
And they drink these waters, although it is dark here
    because it is the night.

I am repining for this living fountain.
Within this bread of life I see it plain
    although it is the night.

XII

Like a convalescent, I took the hand
stretched down from the jetty, sensed again
an alien comfort as I stepped on ground

to find the helping hand still gripping mine,
fish-cold and bony, but whether to guide
or to be guided I could not be certain

for the tall man in step at my side
seemed blind, though he walked straight as a rush
upon his ash plant, his eyes fixed straight ahead.

Then I knew him in the flesh
out there on the tarmac among the cars,
wintered hard and sharp as a blackthorn bush.

His voice eddying with the vowels of all rivers
came back to me, though he did not speak yet,
a voice like a prosecutor's or a singer's,

cunning, narcotic, mimic, definite
as a steel nib's downstroke, quick and clean,
and suddenly he hit a litter basket

with his stick, saying, 'Your obligation
is not discharged by any common rite.
What you must do must be done on your own

so get back in harness. The main thing is to write
for the joy of it. Cultivate a work-lust
that imagines its haven like your hands at night

dreaming the sun in the sunspot of a breast.
You are fasted now, light-headed, dangerous.
Take off from here. And don't be so earnest,

let others wear the sackcloth and the ashes.
Let go, let fly, forget.
You've listened long enough. Now strike your note.'

It was as if I had stepped free into space
alone with nothing that I had not known
already. Raindrops blew in my face

as I came to. 'Old father, mother's son,
there is a moment in Stephen's diary
for April the thirteenth, a revelation

set among my stars – that one entry
has been a sort of password in my ears,
the collect of a new epiphany,

the Feast of the Holy Tundish.' 'Who cares,'
he jeered, 'any more? The English language
belongs to us. You are raking at dead fires,

a waste of time for somebody your age.
That subject people stuff is a cod's game,
infantile, like your peasant pilgrimage.

You lose more of yourself than you redeem
doing the decent thing. Keep at a tangent.
When they make the circle wide, it's time to swim

out on your own and fill the element
with signatures on your own frequency,
echo soundings, searches, probes, allurements,

elver-gleams in the dark of the whole sea.'
The shower broke in a cloudburst, the tarmac
fumed and sizzled. As he moved off quickly

the downpour loosed its screens round his straight walk.

PART THREE:

SWEENEY REDIVIVUS

The First Gloss

Take hold of the shaft of the pen.
Subscribe to the first step taken
from a justified line
into the margin.

Sweeney Redivivus

I stirred wet sand and gathered myself
to climb the steep-flanked mound,
my head like a ball of wet twine
dense with soakage, but beginning
to unwind.
          Another smell
was blowing off the river, bitter
as night airs in a scutch mill.
The old trees were nowhere,
the hedges thin as penwork
and the whole enclosure lost
under hard paths and sharp-ridged houses.

And there I was, incredible to myself,
among people far too eager to believe me
and my story, even if it happened to be true.

Unwinding

If the twine unravels to the very end
the stuff gathering under my fingernails
is being picked off whitewash at the bedside.

And the stuff gathering in my ear
is their sex-pruned and unfurtherable
moss-talk, incubated under lamplight,

which will have to be unlearned
even though from there on everything
is going to be learning.

So the twine unwinds and loosely widens
backward through areas that forwarded
understandings of all I would undertake.

In the Beech

I was a lookout posted and forgotten.

On one side under me, the concrete road.
On the other, the bullocks' covert,
the breath and plaster of a drinking place
where the school-leaver discovered peace
to touch himself in the reek of churned-up mud.

And the tree itself a strangeness and a comfort,
as much a column as a bole. The very ivy
puzzled its milk-tooth frills and tapers
over the grain: was it bark or masonry?

I watched the red-brick chimney rear
its stamen course by course,
and the steeplejacks up there at their antics
like flies against the mountain.

I felt the tanks' advance beginning
at the cynosure of the growth rings,
then winced at their imperium refreshed
in each powdered bolt mark on the concrete.
And the pilot with his goggles back came in
so low I could see the cockpit rivets.

My hidebound boundary tree. My tree of knowledge.
My thick-tapped, soft-fledged, airy listening post.

The First Kingdom

The royal roads were cow paths.
The queen mother hunkered on a stool
and played the harpstrings of milk
into a wooden pail.
With seasoned sticks the nobles
lorded it over the hindquarters of cattle.

Units of measurement were pondered
by the cartful, barrowful and bucketful.
Time was a backward rote of names and mishaps,
bad harvests, fires, unfair settlements,
deaths in floods, murders and miscarriages.

And if my rights to it all came only
by their acclamation, what was it worth?
I blew hot and blew cold.
They were two-faced and accommodating.
And seed, breed and generation still
they are holding on, every bit
as pious and exacting and demeaned.

The First Flight

It was more sleepwalk than spasm
yet that was a time when the times
were also in spasm –

the ties and the knots running through us
split open
down the lines of the grain.

As I drew close to pebbles and berries,
the smell of wild garlic, relearning
the acoustic of frost

and the meaning of woodnote,
my shadow over the field
was only a spin-off,

my empty place an excuse
for shifts in the camp, old rehearsals
of debts and betrayal.

Singly they came to the tree
with a stone in each pocket
to whistle and bill me back in

and I would collide and cascade
through leaves when they left,
my point of repose knocked askew.

I was mired in attachment
until they began to pronounce me
a feeder off battlefields

so I mastered new rungs of the air
to survey out of reach
their bonfires on hills, their hosting

and fasting, the levies from Scotland
as always, and the people of art
diverting their rhythmical chants

to fend off the onslaught of winds
I would welcome and climb
at the top of my bent.

Drifting Off

The guttersnipe and the albatross
gliding for days without a single wingbeat
were equally beyond me.

I yearned for the gannet's strike,
the unbegrudging concentration
of the heron.

In the camaraderie of rookeries,
in the spiteful vigilance of colonies
I was at home.

I learned to distrust
the allure of the cuckoo
and the gossip of starlings,

kept faith with doughty bullfinches,
levelled my wit too often
to the small-minded wren

and too often caved in
to the pathos of waterhens
and panicky corncrakes.

I gave much credence to stragglers,
overrated the composure of blackbirds
and the folklore of magpies.

But when goldfinch or kingfisher rent
the veil of the usual,
pinions whispered and braced

as I stooped, unwieldy
and brimming,
my spurs at the ready.

Alerted

From the start I was lucky
and challenged, always whacked down
to make sure I would not grow up
too hopeful and trusting –

I was asking myself could I ever
and if ever I should
outstrip obedience, when I heard
the bark of the vixen in heat.

She carded the webs of desire,
she disinterred gutlines and lightning,
she broke the ice of demure
and exemplary stars –

and rooted me to the spot,
alerted, disappointed
under my old clandestine
pre-Copernican night.

The Cleric

I heard new words prayed at cows
in the byre, found his sign
on the crock and the hidden still,

smelled fumes from his censer
in the first smokes of morning.
Next thing he was making a progress

through gaps, stepping out sites,
sinking his crozier deep
in the fort-hearth.

If he had stuck to his own
cramp-jawed abbesses and intoners
dibbling round the enclosure,

his Latin and blather of love,
his parchments and scheming
in letters shipped over water –

but no, he overbore
with his unctions and orders,
he had to get in on the ground.

History that planted its standards
on his gables and spires
ousted me to the marches

of skulking and whingeing.
Or did I desert?
Give him his due, in the end

he opened my path to a kingdom
of such scope and neuter allegiance
my emptiness reigns at its whim.

The Hermit

As he prowled the rim of his clearing
where the blade of choice had not spared
one stump of affection

he was like a ploughshare
interred to sustain the whole field
of force, from the bitted

and high-drawn sideways curve
of the horse's neck to the aim
held fast in the wrists and elbows –

the more brutal the pull
and the drive, the deeper
and quieter the work of refreshment.

[109]

The Master

He dwelt in himself
like a rook in an unroofed tower.

To get close I had to maintain
a climb up deserted ramparts
and not flinch, not raise an eye
to search for an eye on the watch
from his coign of seclusion.

Deliberately he would unclasp
his book of withholding
a page at a time and it was nothing
arcane, just the old rules
we all had inscribed on our slates.
Each character blocked on the parchment secure
in its volume and measure.
Each maxim given its space.

Like quarrymen's hammers and wedges proofed
by intransigent service.
Like coping stones where you rest
in the balm of the wellspring.

How flimsy I felt climbing down
the unrailed stairs on the wall,
hearing the purpose and venture
in a wingflap above me.

The Scribes

I never warmed to them.
If they were excellent they were petulant
and jaggy as the holly tree
they rendered down for ink.
And if I never belonged among them,
they could never deny me my place.

In the hush of the scriptorium
a black pearl kept gathering in them
like the old dry glut inside their quills.
In the margin of texts of praise
they scratched and clawed.
They snarled if the day was dark
or too much chalk had made the vellum bland
or too little left it oily.

Under the rumps of lettering
they herded myopic angers.
Resentment seeded in the uncurling
fernheads of their capitals.

Now and again I started up
miles away and saw in my absence
the sloped cursive of each back and felt them
perfect themselves against me page by page.

Let them remember this not inconsiderable
contribution to their jealous art.

A Waking Dream

When I made the rush to throw salt
on her tail the long treadles of the air
took me in my stride so I was lofted
beyond exerted breath, the cheep and blur
of trespass and occurrence.
As if one who had dropped off came to
suspecting the very stillness of the sunlight.

In the Chestnut Tree

Body heat under the leaves, matronly
slippage and hoistings

as she spreads in the pool of the day,
a queen in her fifties, dropping

purses and earrings. What does she care
for the lean-shanked and thorny,

old firm-fleshed Susannah, stepped in
over her belly,

parts of her soapy and white,
parts of her blunting?

And the little bird of death
piping and piping somewhere

in her gorgeous tackling? Surely not.
She breathes deep and stirs up the algae.

Sweeney's Returns

The clouds would tatter a moment
over green peninsulas, cattle
far below, the dormant roadways –
and I imagined her clothes half-slipped
off the chair, the dawn-fending blind, her eyelids'
glister and burgeon.

Then when I perched on the sill
to gaze at my coffers of absence
I was like a scout at risk behind lines
who raises his head in a wheatfield
to take a first look, the throb of his breakthrough
going on inside him unstoppably:

the blind was up, a bangle
lay in the sun, the fleshed hyacinth
had begun to divulge.
Where had she gone? Beyond
the tucked and level bed, I floundered
in my wild reflection in the mirror.

Holly

It rained when it should have snowed.
When we went to gather holly

the ditches were swimming, we were wet
to the knees, our hands were all jags

and water ran up our sleeves.
There should have been berries

but the sprigs we brought into the house
gleamed like smashed bottle-glass.

Now here I am, in a room that is decked
with the red-berried, waxy-leafed stuff,

and I almost forget what it's like
to be wet to the skin or longing for snow.

I reach for a book like a doubter
and want it to flare round my hand,

a black-letter bush, a glittering shield-wall
cutting as holly and ice.

An Artist

I love the thought of his anger.
His obstinacy against the rock, his coercion
of the substance from green apples.

The way he was a dog barking
at the image of himself barking.
And his hatred of his own embrace
of working as the only thing that worked –
the vulgarity of expecting ever
gratitude or admiration, which
would mean a stealing from him.

The way his fortitude held and hardened
because he did what he knew.
His forehead like a hurled *boule*
travelling unpainted space
behind the apple and behind the mountain.

The Old Icons

Why, when it was all over, did I hold on to them?

A patriot with folded arms in a shaft of light:
the barred cell window and his sentenced face
are the only bright spots in the little etching.

An oleograph of snowy hills, the outlawed priest's
red vestments, with the redcoats toiling closer
and the lookout coming like a fox across the gaps.

And the old committee of the sedition-mongers,
so well turned out in their clasped brogues and waistcoats,
the legend of their names an informer's list

prepared by neat-cuffs, third from left, at rear,
more compelling than the rest of them,
pivoting an action that was his rack

and others' ruin, the very rhythm of his name
a register of dear-bought treacheries
grown transparent now, and inestimable.

In Illo Tempore

The big missal splayed
and dangled silky ribbons
of emerald and purple and watery white.

Intransitively we would assist,
confess, receive. The verbs
assumed us. We adored.

And we lifted our eyes to the nouns.
Altar stone was dawn and monstrance noon,
the word rubric itself a bloodshot sunset.

Now I live by a famous strand
where seabirds cry in the small hours
like incredible souls

and even the range wall of the promenade
that I press down on for conviction
hardly tempts me to credit it.

On the Road

The road ahead
kept reeling in
at a steady speed,
the verges dripped.

In my hands
like a wrested trophy,
the empty round
of the steering wheel.

The trance of driving
made all roads one:
the seraph-haunted, Tuscan
footpath, the green

oak-alleys of Dordogne
or that track through corn
where the rich young man
asked his question –

*Master, what must I
do to be saved?*
Or the road where the bird
with an earth-red back

and a white and black
tail, like parquet
of flint and jet,
wheeled over me

in visitation.
Sell all you have

[119]

and give to the poor.
I was up and away

like a human soul
that plumes from the mouth
in undulant, tenor
black-letter latin.

I was one for sorrow,
Noah's dove,
a panicked shadow
crossing the deerpath.

If I came to earth
it would be by way of
a small east window
I once squeezed through,

scaling heaven
by superstition,
drunk and happy
on a chapel gable.

I would roost a night
on the slab of exile,
then hide in the cleft
of that churchyard wall

where hand after hand
keeps wearing away
at the cold, hard-breasted
votive granite.

And follow me.
I would migrate
through a high cave mouth
into an oaten, sun-warmed cliff,

on down the soft-nubbed,
clay-floored passage,
face-brush, wing-flap,
to the deepest chamber.

There a drinking deer
is cut into rock,
its haunch and neck
rise with the contours,

the incised outline
curves to a strained
expectant muzzle
and a nostril flared

at a dried-up source.
For my book of changes
I would meditate
that stone-faced vigil

until the long dumbfounded
spirit broke cover
to raise a dust
in the font of exhaustion.

Notes

'Away from it all': '*I was stretched* . . .' from Czeslaw Milosz's *Native Realm* (University of California Press, 1981), p. 125.

'Chekhov on Sakhalin': Chekhov's friends presented him with a bottle of cognac on the eve of his departure for the prison island of Sakhalin, where he spent the summer of 1890 interviewing all the criminals and political prisoners. His book on conditions in the penal colony was published in 1895.

'Sandstone Keepsake': Guy de Montfort. See *Inferno*, Canto XII, lines 118–20, and also Dorothy Sayers's note in her translation (Penguin Classics).

'The King of the Ditchbacks': see note on Part Three.

Station Island is a sequence of dream encounters with familiar ghosts, set on Station Island on Lough Derg in Co. Donegal. The island is also known as St Patrick's Purgatory because of a tradition that Patrick was the first to establish the penitential vigil of fasting and praying which still constitutes the basis of the three-day pilgrimage. Each unit of the contemporary pilgrim's exercises is called a 'station', and a large part of each station involves walking barefoot and praying round the 'beds', stone circles which are said to be the remains of early medieval monastic cells.

Section II: William Carleton (1794–1869), a Catholic by birth, had done the pilgrimage in his youth, and when he converted to the Established Church he published his critical account of it in 'The Lough Derg Pilgrim' and launched himself upon his most famous work, *Traits and Stories of the Irish Peasantry* (1830–3).

Section V: 'Forty-two years on . . .' Patrick Kavanagh wrote his posthumously published poem, 'Lough Derg', in 1942.

Section VI: 'Till Phoebus . . .', Horace, Odes, Book III, xxi, line 24. 'As little flowers . . .', Dante, *Inferno*, Canto II, lines 127–32.

Section XI: The St John on the Cross poem translated here is 'Cantar del alma que se huelga de conoscer a Dios por fe'.

[122]

Section XII: 'Stephen's diary'. See the end of James Joyce's *Portrait of the Artist as a Young Man*.

PART THREE: SWEENEY REDIVIVUS

The poems in this section are voiced for Sweeney, the seventh-century Ulster king who was transformed into a bird-man and exiled to the trees by the curse of St Ronan. A version of the Irish tale is available in my *Sweeney Astray*, but I trust these glosses can survive without the support system of the original story. Many of them, of course, are imagined in contexts far removed from early medieval Ireland.

S.H.
February 1984

[123]